Independence & Retirement

Pocket Guide

Doug Nordman

The Military Financial Independence & Retirement Pocket Guide

Warning/Liability/Warranty: The author has made every attempt to provide the reader with accurate, timely, and useful information. The information presented here is for reference purposes only. The author and publisher make no claims that using this pocket guide will guarantee the reader greater career, financial, or retirement success. The author and/or publisher shall not be liable for any losses or damages incurred in the process of following the advice in this book.

ISBN: 978-1-57023-320-3 (13-digit); 1-57023-320-9

Library of Congress: 2010941052

Publisher: For information on Impact Publications, including current and forthcoming publications, authors, press kits, online bookstore, newsletters, downloadable catalogs, and submission requirements, visit the left navigation bar on the front page of www.impactpublications.com.

Quantity Discounts: We offer quantity discounts on bulk purchases. Please review our discount schedule on page 60 and at www.impactpublications.com or contact our Special Sales Department at 703-361-7300.

Sales/Distribution: All sales and distribution inquiries should be directed to the publisher: Sales Department, IMPACT PUBLICATIONS, 9104-N Manassas Drive, Manassas Park, VA 20111-5211, Tel. 703-361-7300, Fax 703-335-9486, or query@impactpublications.com.

The Author: Doug Nordman retired at the age of 41 after 20 years with the U.S. Navy's submarine force. He's an enthusiastic surfer, an omnivorous reader, a martial arts student, and a veteran of many chaotic home-improvement projects. After eight years of early retirement he's an expert at answering the question "But what do you DO all day?" He and his spouse, a retired Navy Reservist, are raising a teenager in Hawaii. Life is busier than ever and they can't imagine where they found the time to go to work!

Contents

I Want Financial Independence!

Congratulations – and many thanks for your service! As you approach separation you and your family really need to address this knee-bending question:

What do you want to do with the rest of your life?

Do you want to get on someone else's work treadmill or quit work altogether? Or do you desire to do something more with your life? Maybe you really don't need to pursue a traditional job or career or retire full time. Indeed, as you approach this new season in life at a relatively young age, let's start thinking outside the box by addressing a key concern of military families – financing your long-term future.

> *Given your military training and benefits, you can become financially independent and retire before your golden years!*

The good news is this: Given your military training and benefits, you can become financially independent and retire before your golden years! A military pension boosts your chances for a successful retirement, but it's not essential. Even if you've only completed one enlistment, your skills and discipline will be the foundation for a lifetime of financial security and retirement.

When you're financially independent, you can retire early or work on your own terms. The choice is yours. But the key to retiring early is to **start planning early**. This book will show you how.

Why Are You Still Working?

I tried to answer that question as I thought about retiring from active duty. Everything eventually worked out fine, but the transition had a few speed bumps that we could have avoided with a little more knowledge and better planning.

Life is not only work, power, and riches beyond your wildest dreams – it's earning the **financial independence** to make choices that are right for you. I'm grateful to those who showed me how to achieve this independence. I'd like to honor them by helping others answer their own work- and retirement-related questions.

Plan for the Worst, Hope for the Best

"Why plan for the future? I could be killed tomorrow!" Of course we hope that never happens. But if good training keeps you alive under the military's worst conditions, then why not apply it to the rest of your life? What about **training yourself** financially, mentally, and emotionally for retiring when you want to? You've worked hard to develop your military skills, so why not use those skills to prepare yourself for the rest of your life?

Saving and Investing for Retirement

> *Balance your life and your financial independence and have fun doing it!*

One of the keys to retirement is **savings**. If you blissfully spend your pay, then you will certainly outlive your savings. You may discover a lifetime of occupational drudgery isn't much better than combat! But by saving and investing a little every payday, you'll give **compounding** the chance to work its magic. It's boring, and for the first couple years it's difficult to see the progress. But saving and investing doesn't have to crimp your **lifestyle**. You can balance your life and your financial independence and have fun doing it!

Take Charge of Your Future

Mental preparation for retirement is just as important. Someday you'll be at a tough career spot, perhaps dealing with a family crisis, or facing a retirement deadline that you haven't really thought about. Would you like to be in charge of the retirement decision? As long as you're working, it's worth planning for the worst and hoping for the best. Maybe it's been easier to let the military run your career, but someday (maybe now) you'll be in charge of your future – living the life you really want to live. The earlier you start, the more choices you get to make, and the more fun you'll have doing what you really love to do in the next season of your life!

> *Do what you really love to do in the next season of your life!*

When Should You Stop Working?

What's your future look like? After active duty, will you leave the military for a **bridge career**, will you **semi-retire** to work part-time, or will you **retire early** and never earn a paycheck again?

These are tough retirement issues. The answer is, "It depends." It's not an easy answer, but it's the only one that will help you decide what's best for you. While you're pursuing it, give yourself the option to change your plan. You have time. The skills that employers truly care about (your leadership, your experience, and your ethics) won't go stale. Talk with your family and think about your goals. Don't lock yourself in!

Your **top priority** is your family's **financial independence**. If you haven't achieved that by the time you've left the service, then you'll need to keep working. Your next priority is the **happiness** of you and your family. They may want you around more often and your idea of happiness (and supporting them) may be quite different from theirs. The junction of a career change is a great time to discuss all the options and expectations.

Your feelings and emotions about your career changes will make a big difference in your performance and your health. They're also much more difficult to handle than the mechanics of a transition. On active duty you're surrounded by mentors and peers who can tell you precisely where you need to go and exactly how to get there.

The **best career wisdom** I've ever heard is:

"Do it as long as you're having fun."

Your **peak performance** comes from being **challenged, fulfilled, and happy**. That leads to faster promotions and even better jobs.

Biggest Obstacles Facing All Retirees

All retirees have to accumulate the resources to last for the rest of their lives, but early retirees (before age 65) have two daunting challenges:

1. Paying for health care
2. Contending with decades of inflation

Health insurance is largely a workplace benefit, and many workers feel "locked in" to their jobs by it. Health insurance can be hundreds of dollars per month without an employer's subsidy, and getting coverage for pre-existing conditions is uncertain at the time of writing. The American health care system is the main reason that traditional retirees stay in the workforce until age 65, when Medicare starts to cover much of their health expenses. Even after age 65 retirees still have to contend with rising insurance premiums, higher prescription medication costs, and long-term care concerns.

Inflation is far more insidious. While a health crisis can wipe out a retiree's finances, inflation is at least as deadly because it's hard to notice the corrosive long-term effects. At just four percent a year, a decade of inflation can raise retiree expenses by nearly 50%. **Retirees in their 60s** may only have to contend with two or three decades of inflation, but **retirees in their 40s** will have to survive four or five decades of inflation that could easily triple their expenses!

Two Biggest Military Retirement Benefits

Unbelievably, **TRICARE** is among the nation's premier affordable health care systems. It covers far more for active-duty veterans (and their families) than civilian health insurance – while costing far less. Unfortunately, many veterans don't learn this fact until they leave the service, while others with pre-existing conditions may feel locked into military or civil service in order to be able to afford their health care costs. In 2010 an active-duty retiree paid less than $40/month for comprehensive TRICARE family coverage that, for civilian retirees, would cost hundreds or even thousands of dollars per month.

As good a financial deal as TRICARE may be, the **military pension** is even better! Military veterans can earn a **defined-benefit pension** in an era when employers are moving toward defined-contribution 401(k)s. Despite the risks that we bear to qualify for that military pension, it's paid by one of the world's best-funded institutions with the power to raise its own money.

Not only is the federal government likely to pay military pensions long after corporate pensions hit the skids, that pension includes a **cost of living adjustment (COLA) for inflation.** This is extremely rare in the business world. Military pensions (as well as Social Security) rise each year by the inflation rate measured in the Consumer Price Index (CPI). That index may have its flaws and detractors, but it's the measure that is currently used to track inflation. You may experience a personal inflation rate that's smaller (or perhaps bigger) than the CPI, but **veteran's pensions will keep up with inflation far better than any other pension system.**

Occupations, Bridge Careers, and Avocations

Occupations are the jobs (like a military enlistment) that form careers and avocations. **Careers** are occupations with experience, greater challenges, and more rewards. A **bridge career** bridges the time between your military career and full retirement. (This idea comes from Marc Freedman, author of *Prime Time*.) With many leaving their careers in their 50s or even their 40s, a second career will take willing workers into their 70s.

If you are a veteran in need of a steady income, you may need a bridge career until you're financially independent. After that, it's your choice to seek paid employment or to explore volunteer work or other pursuits.

Avocations are the fascinating careers that you'd tackle for free. When you've reached 20 years of service, you know that you've had a military career. If you wish that you were able to keep going beyond 40 years, your work becomes an avocation. Many lawyers, doctors, and investors practice their craft until they're no longer capable. **Early retirees** claim that early retirement is their avocation.

Veterans may have an additional avocation: a commitment to service. After decades of completing missions and saving lives, taking care of others may be very important to the happiness of veterans.

Another bridge career option is **semi-retirement**. Bob Clyatt, the author of *Work Less, Live More*, sculpts for fun and sells his art to buy more sculpting supplies. You could work seasonally in a specialty or part-time in a new skill. No matter how hard you choose to work at it, semi-retirement affords you the work option to carry your savings through rough markets or to earn more for special expenses.

Getting Advice From Retirees

Studies show that only 15% of the nation's veterans served for at least 20 years. The number who stopped working after military retirement is even smaller. One university survey found that at least 85% of retired officers immediately returned to civilian work. Semi-retirement and bridge careers are far more common, but financial independence is the key to having the choice.

As you seek advice from retirees, **develop your own network**. When shipmates retire, contact them a few months later. They'll be happy to share their new lifestyle and their surprises. Your base's Retired Activities (or Retirement Services) Office is another option. But by far the best place for advice from military retirees is on **Internet discussion boards**. Veterans post at Internet early-retirement discussion boards listed on page 57.

Myths of Military Retirement

Find the logic flaws in these often-heard claims about retirement:

- You're too young; you have so much ahead of you.
- Can't you find a real job?
- Who wants to spend all day golfing?
- You'll lose all your friends!
- But we need you here at the command!
- You'll lose all your contacts, and you won't get a job!
- You'll be so bored.

For explanations behind these myths and more examples, visit: www.the-military-guide.com.

Checklist: "Should I retire?"

- ❏ Value of a military pension: controls health care expenses and hedges against inflation.
- ❏ Retire early, semi-retire, or bridge career?
- ❏ Which do you favor: occupation or avocation?
- ❏ Learn more about your service's Transition Assistance Programs.
- ❏ Consider the benefits of career surveys and assessment tests.
- ❏ Be ready to deal with the myths of early retirement.

How Do You Get Started?

Let's start with the simplest case of financial independence and retirement – retiring directly from active duty and never working again. Later pages will cover how to achieve financial independence without 20 years of active duty, or without even having a military retirement pension.

Before you start checking off the blocks on your command's retirement worksheet, you need to address some larger issues. Be sure to evaluate:

- the timing of your retirement
- the advance planning leading up to that retirement
- your finances

You'll not only need to consider how much you'll be getting in retirement but how much you can spend. Then you'll be ready to start counting down the final days.

Military Retirement Pay

This section summarizes the "High Three" and "Career Status Bonus" systems. For those very few who were in the service before 8 September 1980, see the details at www.the-military-guide.com.

To build your retirement checklist, pick your date and understand how your pension is calculated. Learn the references and make sure they apply to you. The Defense Finance and Accounting Service (DFAS) estimates your retirement pay from your service record, so if you get a different number, there could be an error in your record. **Correct errors *before* you retire – it's much harder to do so after you retire!**

Your retirement pay is calculated from two factors:

1. the date you entered the service
2. your "service multiple"

High Three System

If you entered the service between **8 September 1980 and 31 July 1986,** your pension is based on the average base pay of your final 36 months. The data will be in DFAS's archives and on your old pay statements, so check each against the other to verify your pay record.

Career Status Bonus System

This includes everyone who entered the military **after July 1986**. Originally called "REDUX," it offers either a High Three pension or a $30,000 bonus at the 15th year of service. On page 11 we review why REDUX is a money-losing idea for almost everyone.

Make sure that your **Date of Initial Entrance to Military Service (DIEMS)** is correct. This is usually the date that you were handed your first ID card. It may be earlier if you've had broken service, or if you joined the Reserves and mobilized to active duty, or if you were commissioned through ROTC/service academies. These different dates cause many mistakes at recruiting offices and training commands.

Your **service multiple** is 2.5% times your years of service. If you take the REDUX bonus, your service multiple will be reduced by 1% for each year of service less than 30 years. At 20 years of REDUX your service multiple is only 40% instead of 50%.

Your retired pay is determined by multiplying your pay by the appropriate service multiple. The only pay in the calculation is base pay – not food allowances, housing allowances, uniform allowances, special pay, bonus pay, or anything else.

Your pension may only be 25-40% of your total active duty compensation, but this includes a benefit that counters one of a retiree's biggest challenges: inflation. You receive a **cost of living adjustment** from your first full year of retirement until you die. Most American pensions (if a retiree even has one!) do not have a COLA. Even at a modest annual inflation rate of 3%, after 30 years a fixed pension retains only 40% of its original value, while military retirees may preserve their purchasing power for the rest of their lives.

Is the military pension's COLA really worth the sacrifice? Research has found that pensions of those retiring in 1998 were approximately $300/month less than pensions of 2008 retirees. However, the retirees of '98 were still ahead of those who retired in 2001 (the first year of High-Three retirees) by roughly $100/month. 1973's retirees fared best of all because of high-inflation COLAs in the 1980s. Despite 35 years of active-duty pay raises, the 1973 retirees still received a bit more than the 2008 retirees. Not only did 1973's COLA shield them from 35 years of inflation, but three decades of compounding even put them slightly ahead of the military's current pay system.

Warning: you can wipe out your COLA by taking the REDUX bonus. For $30,000 you agree to a smaller service multiple and give back 1% of your COLA each year between retirement and age 62. At age 62 you'll receive a "catch-up" COLA. Do the math. If you retire at age 37 on 40% of your base pay and give back 1% of your COLA for the next 25 years, then by age 62 your REDUX pension will only be 62% of the High Three pension.

Financial Myths of Retirement

Find the logic flaws in these claims:

- You'll need 83.942% of your pre-retirement income.
- You need rules of thumb for risk, diversification, and asset allocation.
- You can't retire; inflation is too high!
- Your savings need to be absolutely safe.
- Active investing is better than passive investing.
- It's the wrong time to invest in the market.

See the explanations behind these and more examples at:

www.the-military-guide.com.

Retirement Budgeting

The bad news is that retirement will involve a budget. The good news is that this budget is all yours. It can be as simple as the back of an envelope or as time-consuming as a multi-page spreadsheet. The whole point of your budget is to become comfortable with your spending projections and to figure out how much of a retirement investment portfolio you will need to achieve financial independence.

Don't make your budget too confining or too complicated. At this stage you're only figuring out how much you're spending. You're not trying to eliminate waste or to boost savings – those goals come next. Later you'll forecast your retirement expenses, and then you'll calculate how long you'll have to keep earning paychecks. When you've finished with those steps, then you can go back and refine your budget.

The first part of budgeting is easy: **track what you spend**. Don't clamp down on your spending, and especially don't criticize wherever it's spent. Just record it and figure out where it all goes. Create your own system, download software, or save your receipts – but do something. The goal is to determine how much you're spending and to decide if your spending is aligned with your values and desires.

Track your spending for at least a month or two, until you understand where your money is going. While you track your expenses, sort them into meaningful categories. Use software or come up with your own categories, but **distinguish between fixed and discretionary expenditures**. You'll also separate your categories into "pre-retirement" and "retirement" groups.

Retirement Spending

Everyone spends less in retirement, right? Not so fast.

You'll stop spending on uniforms, commuting, childcare, and office expenses. If you're not driving as much, your insurance rates and final costs may drop. Also, your retirement income is taxed at a lower rate and your lower income may put you in a smaller tax bracket.

But you might be traveling more often, dining out several times a week, and spending more money on recreation. If you're relocating, your new home might have higher living expenses. You might decide to pay off the mortgage on your home, but if you move to a new area then you may also have a new mortgage. With all your new free time, you might spend a lot more money on home improvement, landscaping, or hobbies. You may be able to do your own chores and maintenance, but you may need to spend more on supplies.

Make your best guess at your retirement budget. Learn about retirement lifestyles and talk with your family and other retirees. Break your spending estimate down into essential and non-essential groups so that you have more flexibility. You may decide to reduce some non-essential spending to reach your goal earlier. You have plenty of options and the process will go through several iterations.

Once you have a retirement spending plan, you're ready to figure out how much it will cost. If you have enough assets to afford the plan, then you're all set! If not, you have a number of parameters to tinker with. One way or another you'll make this work.

How Much Will I Need Each Year?

The short answer is this: 25 times the amount of your annual spending. If you want to retire on $40,000/year without any pension or other income, then you're going to need a million bucks. If you have a military pension, then your savings need to be about 25 times the gap between your annual expenditures and your military pension. If you have a $30,000 pension then your budget only needs $250,000.

"25x" comes from a number of research studies and retirement calculators. The oldest of them all, the **Trinity Study**, found that the most successful retirement portfolios survived for 30 years by starting at an **annual "safe withdrawal rate" (SWR) of 4%**. That initial withdrawal was raised each year by the rate of inflation. It assumes that you'll consume the principal in those 30 years and that you'll "die broke." If you're concerned about living longer or if you don't want to touch the principal, you may need to save even more!

Or maybe not. The Trinity Study assumed a rigid withdrawal system that ignored actual investment returns, but luckily you can vary your spending. Some retirees cut back in the first few years of retirement until they feel confident enough to loosen the purse strings. Lifestyles change with age. Analysts even claim that spending drops dramatically after age 80, although health care expenses will rise.

No matter how much money you have, if times seem tough then you'll probably defer non-essential expenses or even cut back on your lifestyle. You may even look for part-time temporary work to help nurse a portfolio over the worst of a bear market.

How Much Can I Safely Withdraw and Spend Annually?

A 4% **safe withdrawal rate (SWR)** is the most popular starting point. It's straightforward, has a high success rate, and adjusts for inflation.

Some research claims that a **high-equity portfolio** can last for a longer time or survive a higher withdrawal rate. While high-equity portfolios can be very volatile, they are a good counterbalance to a military pension. If a retiree is willing to risk a slightly higher (yet still remote) possibility of failure, the SWR can be higher. One noted researcher, William Bernstein, even claims that planning for a higher success rate than 80% is unrealistic.

Conservative portfolios (high in bonds and low in equities) can generally only support a lower SWR. Conservative retirement calculators recommend a lower SWR. Some researchers note that retiring into a declining stock market leads to more failures than waiting until the market is recovering. Others have developed complex variable-spending systems with higher initial SWRs.

One author, Bob Clyatt, proposes a simple variable spending system. Instead of Trinity's "4% plus inflation," Bob's system withdraws 4% every year. If the portfolio lost money and next year's 4% is smaller than 95% of the previous year's withdrawal, then the retiree can take 95% of last year's withdrawal. Spending varies with portfolio performance and cuts back during bad years. A retiree may also contemplate part-time work in bad years if spending can't be cut.

The consensus is that 4% is a starting point with many options for higher withdrawal rates.

As always, military retirees have the benefits of a COLA-adjusted pension and much cheaper health care expenses. When coupled with a bridge career, part-time work, or a high-equity portfolio, these advantages will greatly improve portfolio survival through times of greatest inflation. The same benefits should provide a higher success rate in the future and may even allow a higher withdrawal rate. While the debate continues, the consensus is that 4% is a starting point with many options for higher withdrawal rates.

16

Checklist: Retirement Readiness

❏ Carefully consider the timing of your "High Three" or "Career Status Bonus" retirement plans.

❏ Schedule a date for your service's Transition Assistance Program.

❏ Think about possible retirement dates in your career and see how much pension you'd earn in today's dollars. Use this number as the starting point for a retirement budget.

❏ Avoid being trapped by the financial myths of retirement spending (page 12).

❏ Track your spending.

❏ Develop a realistic retirement budget.

❏ Determine whether your retirement budget matches your values and your retirement plans.

❏ Calculate how much you'll need to save in your retirement portfolio. Remember to include military pensions, earnings from a bridge career, other pensions, and Social Security.

❏ Consider how you'll spend your retirement portfolio – whether you'll attempt to live only off its dividends or whether you'll also spend some of the principal.

The Year Before Retirement

Instead of a detailed day-by-day checklist, this section covers the big-picture decisions. Most of them can be revised after retirement, but the more thought and discussion that take place before retirement, the better the choices are likely to be.

File Your Request and Make Your Announcement

While service changes retirement request deadlines and restrictions, it's best to **file your retirement request** a year ahead of your desired retirement date. This should allow ample time to meet all the notification requirements, to turn over to your relief, and to request an appropriate amount of terminal leave. Ideally you've already attended your transition assistance course. If not, this should be done as soon as you can get a date. Another advantage of such early notice is being able to address any medical and dental issues identified during the retirement physical.

Consider your terminal leave requirements very carefully. Depending on your duty location and your relocation plans, you could not only continue to draw your **base pay** but also all **special pay** and **allowances**. At the other end of your range of options, you could also choose to **sell back** the maximum amount of **leave** and remain on duty until the last possible minute. The difference is that selling back leave only earns base pay without any special pay or allowances. The difference may require you to trade several months' additional labor (not leave!) for a cash boost to your retirement portfolio.

Once your chain of command has endorsed your retirement request, it's time to make the announcement you've been waiting for!

What to Tell Everyone

At first it's awkward and even embarrassing. Retirement can actually be threatening to veterans whose occupation may be a big part of their identity. Since identifying with your avocation is part of our career-oriented society, **create a new identity by adding the "retired" word**:

I'm a retired Air Force mechanic.

That may be all the explanation required.

Others may react quite differently. Indeed, **retirement may separate your friends from your co-workers**. A true friend supports you, but a co-worker may not appreciate your goal and could feel that you're abandoning them. Some may seem jealous that you're able to retire and they're not. Many military retirees avoid discussing their plans with their co-workers. They'll talk about going back to school, spending time with family, or even volunteering with charities. While your true friends share your joy, it doesn't mean they want to hear all the details. They may think you'll be tripped up by the retirement myths.

Five-year-old kids may not fully understand retirement. After all you've been working for their whole life. They want to know that you'll be spending time with them. If you're not deploying, they'll happily skip the details!

Adolescents may be a bit more concerned. They know that jobs pay the bills, and they want their allowance. Reassure them that the budget covers everyone while you'll have more time to spend with them. Skeptical kids may have to replay this conversation for months and seek reassurance. (They're also talking it over with their friends, who are reporting this news to their parents.) If you can coach their team or chaperone their field trips, they'll be as enthusiastic about retirement as you are!

Teenagers are a tough sell. They just want their parents to be normal, invisible, and available while they're finding their identity and their independence. They're not going to be enthusiastic about all the time you'll want to spend with them! Your pension may even seem like a lot of money to them (especially if they want a car), and they may not appreciate that it has to last you for the rest of your life. If you want your teens to support your retirement, **you'll have to show them how it's going to improve their life**. Maybe you don't want to move away from their friends until after they've finished high school.

Your parents and in-laws might be even a tougher sell than your teens. In fact, their reaction to your announcement might make you feel like a rebellious teen again. They know all your flaws and weaknesses, and although they might be proud of your accomplishments they won't hesitate to question your judgment. (From their perspective, your spendthrift indolence might put their loved ones on the streets.) If your parents have retired, you should be able to reassure them, especially if you ask for their advice.

If your parents are still working, you can expect resistance. If your parents have avocations of their own or feel that they'll never save enough to retire, you will have difficulty explaining yourself. You and your spouse will have many interesting discussions with them as they attempt to reconcile their standards with yours. The best approach is to emphasize the time you'll be able to spend with your family (including their grandchildren) and to talk about taking a few years off to explore life. Months later they may accept your decision, although privately they may despair that you'll ever be able to hold down a real job again.

Choosing Where to Live

This time you may have a minority vote in the family decision as well as need to consider other family issues:

- Do you want to live near your relatives?
- Do your parents need your support with medical or home care?
- Do you plan to travel long distances to visit family?

Think about these other issues as you pick your area:

1. Select a community that's right for you:

- Should you rent for a while to learn more about the local real estate market?
- Is the neighborhood a great place to raise a family or is it questionable?
- Are there issues relating to traffic, electricity, water, sewage, schools, or zoning?
- What activities do you and your family enjoy, and how close do you want to be to them?

2. Locate near facilities offering key military benefits:

- Do you want to save money by shopping at military commissaries, exchanges, and Class Six Stores? (Important fact: In 2010 the average family of four saved $4,428.24 by shopping in commissaries alone!)
- Do you want to have quick access to major military medical facilities? (If you or a loved one have a chronic health condition, you may not want to drive hundreds of miles for health care.)

3. Consider tax differences and advantages:

- How much will taxes affect your retirement budget?
- What are the state and local tax advantages of moving to Community X rather than Community Y? Or tax advantages of moving to Country X versus Country Y?
- How much are you willing to pay for climate, proximity, and lifestyle?

If you've decided on a **civil service bridge career**, you may choose to work for a state or municipal civil service. You may have a hiring preference (especially with a disability rating) and other benefits.

What about **perpetual travel**? PTs stay weeks or even months in a location, or travel with a motor home. Other options include discount vacation rental condos, trailer parks, or house sitting. RVs are popular but others wait patiently for hops on military flights. Even families can adopt a perpetual-traveler lifestyle with homeschooling or only summer travel. After years of transfers, your kids will easily adapt and be far worldlier than their domestic cousins.

Some PTs take their frugal finances to Mexico or Thailand by becoming **expats**. The most famous expats are the Terhorsts and the Kaderlis, who've been traveling the world since the 1980s. Expat living offers a chance to get to see the "real" country and to know its people. Instead of staying in resorts and hotels, you'll rent city apartments, shop at local stores and eat at local restaurants, and blend into the community. "Going local" means learning to speak the language and to cook the cuisine, celebrating that culture's holidays, understanding how to get around by public transportation, and knowing where to do your laundry. Start with the resources in the "Recommended Reading" list on page 57 and decide whether this is for you.

Technology has revolutionized PT logistics. The lifestyle now includes cell phone roaming, mobile Internet access, and overnight shipping. Mail-forwarding services can send your newspaper or scan the contents and post the images to your Web account. While banks and brokerages may want a more permanent address, PTs also use the mailing address of friends or families and conduct their business online. You will also need to continue to pay your taxes and claim residency in a state. These issues (and other challenges) have already been faced by thousands of PTs who will be delighted to share their advice on the Internet or over a frosty beverage during their next visit to your area.

Checklist: The Year Before Retirement

❑ Verify your service's deadlines for filing your retirement request.

❑ Evaluate your terminal leave requirements.

❑ Consider how you're going to share the news with shipmates, friends, family, and kids.

❑ Where do you want to live? When?

❑ Research military-friendly states.

❑ Consider access to military bases, medical facilities, and other benefits.

❑ Are you a perpetual traveler?

❑ Do you prefer an expatriate lifestyle?

❑ Incorporate technology into a new lifestyle.

Six Months Before Retirement

This pocket guide doesn't have enough space for all the details of a six-month countdown. Visit www.the-military-guide.com or read the companion book, *The Military Guide to Financial Independence and Retirement* (see page 59). This section lists the high points and concludes with the checklist.

Key Decisions

- **Discharge papers: the DD-214** is difficult to prepare and takes a long time to verify that its details are correct. However, once you're out of the service, it's almost impossible to change. Take the time to do it right before you're out.

- **Get started early on medical and dental exams.** You never know what's going to be found and then has to be fixed before you can retire. A little advance preparation will avoid a lot of pain. Make sure your family also uses all of their medical/dental benefits before you retire, and stock up on prescription medications.

- **Take the high road on your checkouts and exit interviews.** This is a tempting time to burn bridges, but you'll have to reflect on these moments for the rest of your life. Think about how you'll respond if you're asked to stay a while longer or to help out while you're on terminal leave. Again, be firm but polite!

- **Consider your retirement ceremony and farewell.** If you don't want a retirement ceremony or a command farewell, state your preferences early and be firm. Your chain of command wants to support you when you've made up your mind.

- **Avoid ambushes and surprises** on your last day. Leave early!

Checklist: Six Months Before Retirement

- ❑ Complete TAP self-assessments and surveys, with spouse if possible, to help you confirm (or change) your retirement plans.
- ❑ Review entire service record for gaps and errors.
- ❑ Review entire medical and dental records for gaps and errors.
- ❑ Request rough draft of DD-214 to add or correct information.
- ❑ Schedule retirement physical (medical and dental).
- ❑ Schedule additional appointments or consultations for family.
- ❑ Schedule appointment with VA counselor if appropriate.
- ❑ Research TRICARE in your retirement location.
- ❑ Obtain supply of prescription medications for you and family.
- ❑ Consider family dental insurance.
- ❑ Update legal documents.
- ❑ Verify all official credit card and travel claims have been paid.
- ❑ Discuss retirement ceremony and farewell with family and co-workers.
- ❑ Plan retirement leave and permissive temporary duty.
- ❑ Consider maximizing that year's TSP and IRA contributions.
- ❑ Review final DD-214.
- ❑ Complete inventories of equipment and classified material.
- ❑ Prepare exit interview.
- ❑ Be ready for questions about working on leave or extending your tour.
- ❑ Prepare recommendations and awards for your personnel.
- ❑ Plan household goods move or request extension in housing.
- ❑ Plan your escape – lay out your schedule for your final day at the command and disappear early.

At the end of your active-duty obligation, should you stay in or get out? The decision is even tougher after the first 10 years: stay in for retirement, or get out now for an easier transition to a bridge career?

Become Knowledgeable

When your head's down in the trenches, doing your best for the mission while preparing for promotions, it's hard to contemplate your alternatives. It's also scary to think about giving up a familiar career and a steady income. The uncertainty of starting over (and perhaps no paycheck for a few months) keeps many veterans on active duty for far longer than they may desire.

It's very easy to serve a decade of active duty in blissful ignorance of the Reserves and National Guard. Some commands never even work with them and there's little reason to teach active-duty personnel about those careers unless it's part of their mission. **Each service's Reserve and National Guard units vary widely in duties, operating tempo, and policies. Get to know your service's branch.**

Members of the Reserves and National Guard can serve on **active duty, drill status, or inactive status**. Drilling is generally one weekend a month with two annual weeks of active duty, but there are many opportunities for longer periods of active duty. Some Reserve and Guard units may deploy every few years, requiring members to serve on active duty for 6-15 months. Other Reservists manage their individual careers and deploy every 5-6 years with or without their unit.

Every drill is worth a point of credit toward retirement, and every day of active duty is worth another point. Members have to earn a minimum annual number of points for a "good year" toward retirement. **Retirement eligibility is reached after 20 good years** (including any active-duty years) and the amount of the pension is based on the point count. Unlike an active-duty retirement, Reserve/NG pensions start payments at age 60. In general, Reservists and National Guard members will earn enough points during their career for a pension of about 15%-40% of active-duty base pay.

The Reserves/NG can be a vast improvement over active duty because you'll have much more control over your assignments and better choices for work/life/family balance. You can decide how much time you want to devote to the military. You can do the minimum drills and mobilizations or go on active duty for months at the same command. You can apply for inactive status – the military's version of unpaid leave. You can apply for schools and extra training or complete online work for additional retirement points. You can complete a minimum assignment with a unit, "homestead" for years, or switch among different billets in the same geographic area. You can be your own best assignment officer.

The Reserve/NG pension starts at age 60, but it's adjusted for both pay raises and inflation. The first pension payment is taken from the latest pay charts. Even though a Reservist may have filed for retirement in 1990 at age 40 and spent 20 years awaiting the start of retired pay, in 2010 at age 60 they'll use the latest pay scale in effect that year. Two decades of pay raises will hopefully have kept up with historic inflation, just as a pension with a cost-of-living-allowance increase will hopefully keep up with future inflation.

Other privileges have very substantial financial benefits. **Reservists/ NG can now purchase TRICARE even when not on active duty.** During the years before age 60 while awaiting retirement pay, they're still eligible for **access to the base and facilities**. They can still use benefits such as a **VA loan and the GI Bill**.

It's easy to transfer to the Reserves from active duty. Veterans can apply months or even years after separating from active duty, and civilians can join without any prior military service.

The Reserves and National Guard can restart your career. When you're unhappy on active duty, it may be extraordinarily difficult to switch career tracks. You'll have to apply to your current career field's personnel managers to leave, and you'll have to apply to another career field's personnel managers to join theirs. You'll be under the gun to learn a new system and to stay competitive for promotion. You might even be expected to start at the bottom of the new ladder, despite all your years of experience (and rank) in your former specialty. If for some reason you were actually passed over for promotion, it's challenging to recover from it and to remain competitive.

The Reserve/NG is a chance to not only change your lifestyle but your military specialty, your rating, your location, your duty station, and your environment. Instead of working hours of overtime for months to stay ahead of the pack, you can find a niche where you're more competitive. Reservists who don't promote will continue to be considered at selection boards and may even be permitted to remain in a drilling status, accumulating retirement credit even though they may not be paid for their drills.

Avoid These Civilian-Military Pitfalls

You can balance a civilian career with the military commitment if both sides can **make accommodations**. Sometimes the arrangement is harmonious, especially if your career is in federal civil service or a military-support field. Other times you'll be tugged in different directions – particularly if you're a small business owner or a self-employed entrepreneur. Federal laws (and many states) protect your veteran's rights to employment and job status, but there are subtle variations of cooperation, compliance, and enforcement. When your upcoming National Guard deployment may affect your civilian career, it's important to let your co-workers know. You don't want your occasional absence to cause a disruption and leave behind feelings of confusion or betrayal. If an adversarial relationship develops, you're sure to be on the losing side.

The most important aspect of balancing the two lifestyles is a detailed knowledge of your **civilian-military leave policies**. Your military chain of command will know what you rate, but your civilian boss will probably need your constant support and education. You may be able to take a leave of absence from your civilian job or meet your military requirements on weekends and holidays. You may also be required to use vacation days to complete your Reserve duties. It's an awkward compromise and it's not always fair.

You and the Reserves/NG can also **support your employer**. Schedules and deployments are usually set months in advance and can help you coordinate with your civilian staff. If your employer is particularly supportive of your Reserve commitments, nominate them for an award! Advertise every win-win situation. Show off your military skills whenever they can be applied to your civilian job, and look for opportunities to use your civilian skills in your military leadership and management. Your experience in each world may help you get promoted in the other.

Family life is another challenge. If you're drilling, you'll miss a family weekend every month, perhaps with travel, and you'll be working at least two weeks a year in uniform, perhaps with more travel. National

Guard units occasionally go on travel to train for weeks and then deploy for months. If you're raising young children or spending extra time with aging parents, then you may have to transfer to inactive status for a few years until you can be flexible and mobile again. While you're deployed, spouses may have to deal with the military and health care bureaucracies on their own. It's important to make sure you both know how to find the information, assistance, and benefits that you've earned.

Retire Right Now on Reserve/NG Savings

One of the biggest advantages of the Reserve/NG is an inflation-adjusted pension at age 60. Civilian retirees, if they even have a pension, may not only have to wait years, but they may also have to worry that the company won't survive to pay the "guaranteed" pension. A military pension is even more highly rated than an insurance company's annuity, and you don't have to worry whether the insurance company will be able to make good on its future claim. A military pension is as close as you can get to a guaranteed stream of income.

The key to retirement as a Reservist/NG is planning your retirement finances around multiple streams of income. By the time you request retirement (awaiting pay), you'll have several different forms of savings. In addition to the pension at age 60, you'll also have your military **Thrift Savings Plan (TSP)** account, as well as personal IRAs and taxable investments. If you're in the federal civil service, you'll have a second TSP account. If you're employed by a corporation, you'll probably have another tax-deferred savings account – a **401(k)** – as well as other forms of deferred compensation. And if you're self-employed, there are several other ways to save through tax-deferred accounts.

Your challenge is to live off your savings until the tax-deferred accounts are available and until the Reserve/NG pension starts. The advantage of the pension is its known starting date, its inflation adjustment, and its high probability of payment. Your other savings may only have to bridge the gap between your retirement request and the start of your pension. You won't have to worry about outliving your money – only about making it last until the pension begins. In addition to spending down your taxable accounts, you can also tap your tax-deferred accounts if necessary and, under some conditions, even without penalty. If savings won't stretch to cover the whole gap between retiring and receiving a pension, then annual income can be augmented from part-time work or a civilian bridge career.

The planning and calculations may seem complicated or even overwhelming, but today's **retirement-planning software** is tremendously flexible at projecting multiple streams of income over an entire retirement. The "Recommended Reading" section on page 57 has more information about different programs and their advantages.

Checklist: Reserves and National Guard

☐ Learn as much as you can about the Reserves and National Guard. You may make a life-changing choice.

☐ Leverage your Reserve/NG career by applying your training and experience to your civilian career.

☐ Leverage your Reserve/NG earnings by maximizing your tax-deferred savings, especially in the TSP.

☐ Consider other tax-deferral savings plans such as:

- individual IRA
- 401(k) – if with corporate employer

☐ Plan your retirement around multiple streams of income starting at different ages. Investigate tracking software and retirement calculators that explore different scenarios.

This section pertains to life after your military service ends. Maybe your pension doesn't cover all of your expenses. Maybe you're not getting a military pension at all, let alone low-priced health care. Maybe you decided not to stick around for 20 years, or the Reserves/NG didn't work out.

At this point it can be hard to see the benefit of your military service, and you may even feel that you're no better off than a civilian! But keep reading – lots of veterans have figured out how to retire early even without military benefits, and you can too.

Retiring Only on Your Own Savings

This pocket guide has started with the "simplest" finances of military early retirement (staying on active duty for at least 20 years) to the most difficult (leaving after your first obligation ends). Financially, the best choice is staying on active duty until you are eligible to retire.

But statistics confirm that is certainly not the easiest choice. The vast majority of veterans don't even stay for 10 years, let alone a career. **Only 15% of all veterans qualify for a pension** (that includes Reserves/NG as well as active duty) and some services have an even lower retirement population.

So, while resigning may seem to be the most difficult path to retirement, it's by far the most common one. Salary and bonuses are always helpful, but **career satisfaction and quality of life** are much more important. Only you and your family can decide what's best for you, and you may find yourself saying, "Well, it's only money."

The most powerful tools of a military retirement are low-cost health care and an inflation-adjusted pension. How in the world can a veteran reach early retirement without either of them? **It's not as easy, but it can be done.** Civilians may not have these military options, but there are solutions. Some companies still pay fixed pensions and offer subsidized health care. Other retirees save aggressively and buy their own health care insurance until they're old enough for Medicare. A few retirees depend on a "multiple streams of income" approach. Still others bridge the gaps with part-time employment or extraordinary frugality.

Transferable Military Values

The military can make it hard for veterans to appreciate how favorably their discipline, ethics, and skills compare to those of the civilian workforce. The military is a dangerous career, budgets are tight, and risk-taking may be discouraged. The chain of command can impose layers of bureaucracy in every direction and smother initiative. Military bearing and uniform appearance are under constant scrutiny. Supervisors and inspection teams relentlessly point out the slightest flaws in every aspect of duty. Performance assessments regularly give veterans the impression that they're barely capable of handling their current rank, let alone being promoted. It's no surprise that some can be made to feel as if they're worthless and inadequate!

Many veterans are surprised at how well their military skills transfer to a civilian career. Employers are happy to hire workers who can show up on time and be ready to work safely. Ethics and honesty, always a military expectation, can be a welcome surprise to a civilian employer. Veterans are used to accomplishing miracles with few resources and are quite accustomed to being put on the spot by supervisors, co-workers, or clients. Workplace crises and even emergencies are no problem compared to a combat zone. Civilian budgets and supervision may still be tight, but veterans have long ago learned to work the system to reward initiative, stamina, and discipline.

Veterans have learned how to make tough decisions, develop a plan, and have the stamina to carry it out. Very few people in their 20s can lead dozens of experienced workers, care for large quantities of expensive and dangerous equipment, and execute a six-figure budget. The same skills and experience will help you plan and execute your retirement, and you'll have the self-discipline to reach your goals.

The Safe Withdrawal Rate (SWR)

Here's a brief summary of the four most popular savings and withdrawal options:

1. The 4% rule. The Trinity Study showed that a retiree's portfolio almost always lasts for 30 years if retirees start their first year by spending up to 4% of that portfolio, and then raise each year's withdrawals by the rate of inflation. Some principal is consumed, and the portfolio could run out after a string of very bad years

The Trinity paper spawned an entire business of SWR analysis. Is it really 4%? What about 35 or even 50 years of early retirement? How bad can inflation get? What if we spend less money some years? What else can we squeeze out of better data and more powerful analysis? It turns out that variable spending can greatly improve on the 4% SWR.

2. The dividend rule. Conservative retirees spend only what their portfolios earn from dividend-paying stocks, high-quality bonds, rental real estate, and CDs. Spending may be limited by last year's dividend income, or CDs might be spent during a recession to allow stock and bond dividends to recover. To preserve purchasing power, dividends will have to rise at least as fast as inflation. The SWR is less than the portfolio's total dividend rate and almost always less than 4% per year. Spending may fluctuate with the economy or inflation but the portfolio never runs out of money because principal is never consumed. However, the lower SWR requires a larger portfolio than the 4% rule does, which usually means saving more or working longer.

3. **Multiple streams of income.** This option has almost as many variations as the 4% rule. Some retirees **work part-time** at their avocations (or develop new ones) for the rest of their lives. Some **work a few mornings a week or seasonally** for special spending occasions, or when their portfolio falls below a warning line. **Rental real estate** is a popular way to create a stream of reliable income with fewer working hours. Finally, many veterans combine a military pension with **civil-service or civilian pensions** and their savings to bridge the gap to Social Security.

4. **Frugality.** These retirees start with a bare-bones survival budget and add in various "luxuries" from their portfolio's performance or their willingness to work for extra income. Before they'll seek work, however, they'll happily cut waste or reduce expenses. They're more focused on the challenges of their lifestyle than its luxuries (or lack thereof). They might reduce expenses by living overseas, in a recreational vehicle, or even on a small boat. While very few frugal retirees may occasionally cross the line into deprivation, nearly every early retiree practices some aspect of this technique.

Retirement finances will almost always be split among all four options. Many retirees still fondly recall the day in their working years when they updated their net worth spreadsheet and realized that they had enough to meet the 4% rule. Others had a lifestyle epiphany and began aggressively cutting expenses, saving every spare penny, and carefully tracking their progress. A few saved enough to pursue their avocation and happily take whatever payments come their way. A very small number will spend years or decades traveling the world's bargain countries or living a bare-bones lifestyle before settling down to a more traditional retirement in their dream location.

20 years of active duty may seem like the simplest option for a COLA pension and cheap health care, but lifestyle and family may dictate otherwise. An impending transfer may force an abrupt transition decision. The Reserves and National Guard offer a wide variety of options for work-life balance, but success depends on having complementary military and civilian careers that allow switching between the two.

> *20 years of active duty may seem like the simplest option for a COLA pension and cheap health care, but lifestyle and family may dictate otherwise.*

Completely quitting the military is another option. It offers transition benefits and the GI Bill to build on years of training and practical experience that is valued by all employers.

You will find your own path. And when you do, you can share your wisdom with the future retirees who are reading the next chapter.

Checklist: Other Paths to Retirement

❑ Learn about your transition benefits. You never know when you'll need them.

❑ Get as much training and college education as you can, especially online or nights/weekends. You never know when you'll need these skills for your own transition.

❑ Build your savings. You'll need the funds to pay your transition expenses and also to build your early retirement portfolio.

❑ Seek out investment opportunities. Educate yourself and find out what works for you: traditional mutual funds, picking stocks, investing in real estate, or starting your own business.

❑ Enjoy your career as long as you're feeling fulfilled and rewarded. You might stay on active duty all the way to retirement, or the fun might stop before you finish your first obligation. Be ready to make the transition and find your own path.

We're Just Starting Out...
How Do We Get There?

The military will tell you about financial responsibility, and you'll be offered ways to save for financial independence, but **you'll have to do your own retirement planning.** You'll have to apply the resources in ways that the Department of Defense never imagined. The decisions you make in your 20s and even 30s can have a large impact on your financial independence in your 40s or 50s.

Many decisions will be made for you during your military career: duty stations, training, deployments, and how to handle combat. You'll also be making your own life decisions: a college degree, finding a spouse or partner, buying a house, starting a family, and leaving the military for a bridge career or early retirement. Finances may not always be your top priority. **Life decisions like education, marriage, and family involve far more important considerations than "just" money.** But if your choices happen to give you a head start on financial independence, then time and compound interest will take care of the rest.

Although the military may happily subsidize your lifestyle with base housing, savings-plan deductions, and other benefits, you'll need to take the reins and do your own planning. It might be better in the long run to save additional funds in taxable accounts, or to build equity by owning an off-base home, or even to invest in rental property. Your basic military skills (and the transition assistance programs) will help you start a bridge career, but you'll have to use your own initiative and planning to achieve a satisfactory retirement.

If you consistently make your military career the most important aspect of your life, then those life decisions may be made for you by the military. That's not a bad thing, especially if you're a great leader who makes the military your avocation, but the military may not always reward your devotion in the manner you'd intended. As we have already said, the vast majority of veterans enjoy the military as a profession for only a few years. Very few stay for 20 years. The **work/life balance is a perpetual struggle,** and it's important to pay attention to the life opportunities around you. If the military is not your avocation and you'd rather make your own life decisions, you'll need to stay alert for opportunities that will lead you to financial independence. We'll talk more about dealing with the "fog of work" later in this chapter, **but the first step is to start saving**.

Start Saving Now

All the financial retirement media boils down to one piece of advice: **save money**. Your retirement portfolio depends on the amount of money saved and the length of time that it grows. If you save more money, you won't need as much time. You probably won't save hundreds of thousands of dollars a year, so the most important factor becomes time: start saving **now**. Even $50 per paycheck starts a habit that will grow for the rest of your career.

The race to retirement is a marathon, not a sprint, and you'll start at a slower pace. Most military retirees will grow their portfolios for a minimum of 20 years. The first year or two of paychecks may only support a small amount of savings, but once the saving habit is established, it's easier to apply it through every pay raise and promotion.

The "savings mindset" is far more important than a dollar amount or the percentage of a paycheck. The key is to spend money only on the things that add value and joy to your life and to save for the goals that will add even more value. Spending a dollar today may bring a few happy moments or months of pleasurable use, but that dollar invested at 4% for 20 years will more than double in worth. The spending question is not "Can I afford it?" The saving questions are "Which do I value more? Do I want to enjoy this today, or do I want to save the money for retirement? Do I want to work 16 weeks to pay for this, or would I rather save the money for retirement?"

Focus on the big financial decisions that have a big impact on your budget. The media claims that the "latté factor" adds up when a small daily expense is invested and compounded for 20 years. However, this is such a small expense that you're unlikely to avoid spending it and even less likely to put it into savings. Why suffer needlessly?

Instead of agonizing over small daily expenses, consider your fundamental lifestyle choices that will have a large impact on your savings. Start with housing: do you want to rent, or own a luxury condo in the expensive part of town, or would a modest home (closer to work) be better? If you're going to spend most of the next year in the desert or at sea, do you really want to pay for costly storage? If you're living closer to work, could you spend less time commuting and maybe even bicycle or walk? Do you really need a hot sports car or a big truck? These big decisions will save you hundreds of dollars a week.

Consider what's important in your life and **make your spending match your values**. You want to save money, invest it, and grow it to support your lifetime spending. The only way to understand your expenses is to track your spending. The only way to calculate how much you'll need is to know how much you're spending. The only way to track your progress is to track your spending.

Track your progress any way you can. Retirees use just about every method – expensive budgeting/accounting programs, free software, spreadsheets, handwritten notebooks, or even cash in envelopes for different spending categories. You have to develop a habit that works for you – saving receipts during the day and entering them onto a computer that night, entering purchases on your smart phone, or simply spending until that envelope runs out of money. Find the method that makes you feel good about your progress.

Frugal Living is Not Deprivation

The military teaches everyone how to live an extraordinarily frugal lifestyle. At some point you've lived in a very small room with a narrow bed and little storage. Maybe all your possessions had to be carried on your back. Food was mass-produced, or perhaps you missed an occasional meal. Entertainment was rudimentary – no high-definition satellite TV or Internet access, let alone clubbing downtown!

Unfortunately the military's frugality usually crosses the line to deprivation. **Frugality is just simple living that avoids waste.** Early retirement benefits from frugality, but it doesn't require deprivation.

The difference comes from your personal values – everyone has a line that they choose not to cross. Frugality feels good and makes you enthusiastic about your goals. It's a challenge and you feel like a winner. Frugality matches your values with savings for financial independence. **Deprivation, however, rarely matches your values and makes you feel poor.** It's always doing without for a higher priority, willingly or not. You may be making progress, but it's hard and you will not feel good about it. Prolonged deprivation leads to unhappiness.

A materialistic society does not always value frugality. The difference is how you feel about it. If you're amused by shipmates' comments, then your frugality reflects your values and your net worth. If you're "left out" or feeling bad, you've probably crossed the line into deprivation. **Many people see frugality as tedious labor from the Great Depression, but it depends on what you value.** Cooking from scratch is more effort, but you may enjoy the value you derive from your own creative, high-quality meals. But while you're quite happy to save money by eating at home, you may draw the line at rinsing and re-using plastic bags. It doesn't matter to you that others see this as recycling. You may not be willing to expend your labor on that goal.

Frugality is not an all-or-nothing lifestyle. Choose the techniques that bring value to your routine. You may enjoy the daily challenge or you might decide to only be extra frugal after an emergency expense. You may adopt just one or two ideas (like bicycling for short trips) and then expand them (commuting or taking a bicycle trek for your next vacation). Monitor your spending, decide what's worth your effort, and change your habits as necessary.

Frugal zealots may be accused of taking advantage of others. There's nothing wrong with ordering the restaurant's water or smaller or cheaper menu items. However, if you're sharing the bill, do your part. It's wrong to help yourself to food that you're not paying for, or to skimp on the tip. **Frugality is not tricking others into paying for you – that's being cheap.**

Families can easily adopt frugality and raise children with strong life skills. If you attempt to impose deprivation on your family, however, you'll be facing rebellion in the ranks. People will have to either choose to upgrade their lifestyle or change their values until deprivation eases up to frugality. If you're imposing deprivation on your family, you may not get the cooperation you expect. Be patient and be ready to compromise.

Payroll Deductions

"Pay yourself first." "Out of sight, out of mind." "You can't spend it if you don't have it." Those sound bites may be annoying, but they're right. Frugality and budgeting help you align your spending with your values. Saving has to be a top priority, or you'll never save enough to let compounding work its retirement magic.

Instead of facing a spending decision every day, set a savings goal and then put it on autopilot. Build your budget, decide how much you can afford to save, then make it happen automatically. Maximize your contributions to the Thrift Savings Plan. Send an allotment to a fund company for your IRA. When the rest of your paycheck hits your checking account, have an auto-transfer send some of it to your taxable investments. Sweep more of it to a savings account and leave only that month's budget in your checking account. When the money's whisked away, it's easier to make the rest last until the next payday. You won't be tempted to "adjust" the spending priorities. Whatever savings goal you choose, let technology take care of it for you every payday.

A huge opportunity comes with annual pay raises, longevity pay raises, special pay, bonuses, and promotions. Send these windfalls straight to savings and learn to live without them. Inflation may chew on your budget, and a growing family will always be more expensive. But when a raise comes, try to raise your savings rate first by saving 80% of the extra pay. If it's causing too much pain, you can back off to 60%. It's far less painful to ease up on the savings rate than to try to raise it!

Thrift Savings Plan, IRAs, and Others

Now that you've saved it, where do you put it? Two basic concepts should guide all of your investment decisions: **minimize expenses and minimize taxes**. There are dozens of techniques and asset classes, but studies prove that these are the two most critical factors.

The less you pay in fees, the more money you have compounding for you. **Invest your pay in the tax-deferred Thrift Savings Plan first, before the pay is subject to income tax, so that you can invest more.** The longer you avoid paying taxes on profits, the more you keep and the longer it can compound.

The Thrift Savings Plan is a tax-deferred account of the world's largest index funds with the world's lowest expenses. Your payroll contributions come from before-tax money (up to the legal limit) and you don't have to pay taxes until you withdraw them. Better still, the expense ratio was under 0.02% in 2008-09. (No other mutual fund comes close.) Best of all, you can set it up online and put it on autopilot.

After you reach the TSP's annual contribution limits, invest in your Individual Retirement Arrangement. IRAs are similar to the TSP because they grow tax-deferred and have very specific withdrawal rules. The difference is that you have to select your own IRA account custodian (financial company) and choose from a much wider range of assets and funds. IRAs have lower contribution limits and higher expenses than the TSP, but you have more control and more choices.

When you're in your 20s and 30s, focus on building the accounts. Let them compound for at least 20 years. Don't worry about future withdrawals. There are penalty-free methods of borrowing or withdrawing money if necessary, but your goal is to compound them. Your retirement planning will include other assets that you'll spend first.

The TSP and IRAs are the only tax-deferred savings plans available to the vast majority of veterans. However, more money can be saved in **taxable accounts**. ("Taxable" because you pay annual taxes on distributions and sales.) Although profits are taxable, the goal is still to maximize savings while minimizing expenses and taxes.

Taxable accounts are as simple as opening a savings account with a credit union, and as complicated as a brokerage account. The simpler your plan, the easier it is to execute. Use a mutual-fund company (such as Fidelity Investments or Vanguard) to buy low-cost index funds. Whatever asset classes and funds you buy, your focus should be on saving as much as possible for as long as possible.

After setting up TSP and IRA contributions, a veteran's **next priority should be funds for emergencies and short-term goals**. An "emergency" is a car repair, a broken toilet, or a short-notice plane ticket to help a loved one. Emergencies are not new trucks, new clothes, or concert tickets – those are short-term goals. A short-term goal is a savings plan for anything that meets your values and could happen in the next few years. It could also include a house down payment, college tuition, a wedding, or even a fantasy vacation. Set savings goals for both entertainment and lifestyle upgrades.

The emergency and short-term funds should have no risk of loss. The most popular account for these funds is a **certificate of deposit (CD)**. The best rates are usually at **credit unions**. The size of the fund is up to you and your goals – anywhere from one to eight months' pay for an emergency fund. The fund may need to be bigger if you're transferring to a new duty station or leaving the military, but as long as you expect a paycheck, you can minimize your emergency fund.

You pay a price for financial safety. CDs are insured against loss, but returns are lower than investments that have a risk of loss. It can really hurt to park your money in a 1% CD when every other investment seems to be paying 6%, and it's tempting to chase the higher yield. **Don't do it.** You're saving this money for emergencies and for important short-term goals. Pursue higher yields in the TSP, IRAs, and long-term taxable accounts where the money can stay invested for decades. A CD earns a lower return, but its payoff comes when you need the money. It's much easier to sleep at night if you know that you can cover an emergency without having to max out a credit card or get a payday loan. And although a CD may only pay 1%, the real savings comes from the cash discounts. You want to be the buyer who asks for a lower cash price, not the desperate seller with an emergency.

Once you've planned your savings for emergencies and short-term goals, set up your final taxable account for long-term investments. These funds can be used for far-off goals that won't be needed for at least five years (house down payment) and possibly even longer (kid's college tuition, retirement). Although they're not tax-deferred like the TSP or an IRA, taxes and expenses can still be reduced by using funds that trade infrequently (low turnover) and that minimize taxable distributions. The most popular asset classes in this account are low-cost stock and bond index funds.

Real Estate: Renting Versus Buying

Everyone knows a military real-estate mogul. They're always looking at properties, working on their home, and maybe even acting as landlords. For them, real estate is more than a hobby – it's an avocation.

These enthusiasts are handling assets worth five or even ten times their annual pay by using leverage. Very few veterans actually own their homes debt-free because it takes years of saving and most military will move at least a half-dozen times during a 20-year career. Instead they're buying homes with a 5%-20% down payment from their own money and borrowing the rest. They're paying their mortgage from their salary, housing allowance, or a tenant's rent. If the real estate market is doing well when it's time to sell, then their leverage bet pays off handsomely. If the real estate market is flat, though, they'll lose money on the expenses. People don't talk about their real-estate failures, either, so the silent losses make property ownership seem like a guaranteed success.

You'll confront the same decision with every transfer: live on base, rent, or own a home. **Each choice has its own merits, and they're not always financial.** At some assignments you may be required to live on base, while U.S. locations may have waiting lists for base housing. You may prefer to live on base if you're "on call" or you may want better schools for your kids. If you expect to be at a duty station for a number of years, you may be tempted to buy your own place.

Before you run to town with your housing allowance, though, **consider how this spending matches your lifestyle and your values**. Is the base housing better or worse than the surrounding community? Will you have a better commute or will you be spending an hour a day in traffic? How much time will you be spending in your house, especially if you're deploying soon? Where will your kids have better schools? Living out in town may put you among locals and "real" life, but it may also deprive your family of the special community of military families coping with shared sacrifices. It may also make it harder to find repair help and contractors. Are you a "house person" willing to tackle your own projects? Would you rather let a landlord take care of the home you're renting? Do you want to be responsible for your own maintenance and repairs, or would you rather let contractors fix your base home while you spend your time doing things that you value more?

Once you've settled on your values and lifestyle, the challenge becomes using your housing allowance as effectively as possible. You're not required to spend every penny of it. You might be able to find a place that costs only 90% of the allowance, or even 75%. Maybe it makes more sense to buy a duplex and rent out half of it while living in the other side. Consider all of the costs, not just the rent or the mortgage. "Other" costs include down payments, deposits, mortgage insurance, financing fees, closing costs, utilities, community association fees, escrow accounts, homeowner's or renter's insurance, property taxes, and commuting. They may not seem like much, but they quickly add up. There are tax advantages to owning a home, but the expenses can be far more costly.

While real estate (and its leverage) may seem to be the perfect path to riches and retirement, **you might not be able to afford the risk of a loss**. Millions of unfortunate homeowners have learned that real estate prices can go down as much as they go up, and financial leverage is not a good idea if you can't find a tenant. When you're also at risk of moving every few years, buying/selling a home is a high-cost transaction that eats into profits. Being a long-distance landlord is begging for trouble, and you may not have enough rent to be able to afford a full-time property manager. Rental losses will wreck a veteran's investment portfolio faster than almost any other financial calamity.

Moving off-base is not a simple decision. Even if it seems to be the right choice for you and your family, renting or owning is another complex lifestyle/financial decision. Once you've decided those questions, then you still have to ensure that your housing costs are within your means and that you're saving the excess. Finally, consider whether you want to add to all your other lifestyle burdens by tackling the responsibility and risk of being a landlord. While it sounds like a no-brainer to buy that duplex and rent out the other side, the actual process is more complex (and financially treacherous) than it may appear.

If you're reasonably confident you'll be spending the majority of your career at that location, or at least willing to be a long-distance landlord even while you're stationed somewhere else, then you'll likely earn a profit. However, depending on local conditions and the economy, **you might have more lucrative places to invest your money** – and index mutual funds are a lot less work. If you're buying real estate just because it seems like the quickest way to get rich, then you may also learn that leverage can work against you. Many have succeeded, but a significant minority have failed, so research the costs and invest in the assets that fulfill your values. If you're absolutely fascinated by the idea of owning a home and devoting the extra "sweat equity" to the landlord lifestyle, then hopefully you'll succeed!

Tailor Your Portfolio to Your Military Pay

Moshe Milevsky's book *Are You a Stock or a Bond?* claims that active-duty military can invest much more aggressively. Every worker's "human capital" has the lifetime potential to earn different amounts of money with varying reliability. Some enjoy continuous employment, like civil servants and university professors, with lower incomes yet good retirement benefits. Their income is like a bond.

Other occupations, like Wall Street financier or professional sports, can generate huge payoffs in bonuses or options – but their employment is unreliable. They can be laid off during any recession, or a single injury can end their career. They might earn much more but their income is unpredictable and they have to depend on their own retirement plans. Their income volatility resembles that of a penny stock.

Veterans' "human capital" can earn millions from recruiting to retirement. Their training, skills, and experience are converted to investment dollars plus retirement and health care benefits. In combat zones their pay and benefits rise to cover the higher risks. **A veteran's income is like a high-quality government bond.**

According to Milevsky, on active duty your investment asset allocation can shift to stocks because your human capital already resembles bonds. You'll still have an emergency fund and save for goals like buying a home, but you don't need to own more bonds. As long as you're earning active duty or drill pay, you can take extra risks with your TSP and IRAs for higher returns.

If you have a military pension, you can also invest aggressively. **A military pension is one of the world's best annuities from inflation-adjusted bonds.** Offset that huge bond allocation by investing the rest of your portfolio in equities and real estate. The higher long-term return can greatly speed your retirement.

There's an emotional problem with this logical plan: your high-equity portfolio's higher long-term return has a much higher short-term volatility. If you don't need to sell the assets within five years, and if you can sleep at night despite large swings in their value, then you can invest more aggressively. Everyone swears that they'll tolerate volatility, but no one enjoys losing money. Panicking and selling equities at the bottom of a bear market will quickly wipe out years of extra gains. **If a 25% drop causes enough emotional stress to abandon your plan, hold fewer equities or more real estate for lower volatility.**

If your Reserve/National Guard career reached retirement with a smaller pension, or if you retired with no pension at all, then consider using a portion of your savings to buy a no-frills fixed annuity that supplies a portion of your retirement income. Annuities earned a bad reputation in the 1990s for their high commissions and expenses, but even Milevsky has been impressed by their recent improvements. Insurers are more conservative in their annuity risk, and their products are more likely to be backed by a strong company. Their annuities aren't as highly guaranteed as a military pension, but they'll support a "basic necessity" lifestyle. Keeping a few years' expenses in money markets and CDs will allow you to ride out the worst of a bear market's volatility while remaining confident that your overall portfolio has the resiliency (and the time) to recover from the financial roller coaster.

The "Fog of Work"

Why aren't there more military retirees? Why is this so hard? The goal takes dedication, but a major disruption is the "fog of work."

For those who haven't had to study military strategy, von Clausewitz's famous quote is "All action takes place ... in a kind of twilight, which like a fog or moonlight, often tends to make things seem grotesque and larger than they really are." The "fog of work" is the perfect retirement problem!

When you're working, you're alert for opportunities and striving to get ahead. If you don't act, you might miss a great chance to improve your life or your net worth. If you're not happy with your current situation, step back, calmly consider the pros and cons of change, and make a rational decision. Sounds simple, right?

But most of us are overwhelmed with work. When we're not at work, we're getting ready to go to work or taking care of the chores and childcare that support our work. At night we're still slumped on the couch watching TV comedies about work or thinking about going back to work. Even our kids grow up, finish school, and go to work.

We've planned most of our life around work. We do a lot of work, whether it's productive or not. But when do we plan our **life**?

The real problem is that we're too busy working and the planning is too hard. Maybe we're afraid to plan. Investments have to recover from the recession, or we have no idea how much we spend now or how much we need. If people did the research, many would be surprisingly happy with the results. Yet even then their reaction is, "But what will I do all day?!?" Another planning problem? Maybe the fog clears for a few minutes and you realize that your plan needs a change. But whoops, the phone is ringing and there's new email. And soon the fog of work returns you to its smothering embrace....

Clausewitz's "fog of war" teaches military commanders to plan, move, and adapt. There's never enough data to fully reveal the situation. There's never time to develop a **perfect** plan. The longer they delay, the quicker the enemy wins. Their only solution is to pull their heads out of the tactical situation for a minute, stop waiting for more data, and see where they can go now. Break free.

It's the same in the "fog of work." **People have to find a break from their daily busy-ness to learn how to reach financial independence.** They have to practice retirement – try just "being" for a while instead of "doing." If veterans had a two-month sabbatical, how many would go back to work? If we had the confidence (and assets) to stop working, we'd rediscover our other interests. We'd do whatever we wanted without contracts or deadlines.

There's only one solution: whisk away the fog of work. Take the time off. Rest up. Heads will clear after a week of naps, leisurely walks, and family chats. Focus on the future and plan how to get there. Without the fog of work, we'd look at the office and think "What a bunch of toxic waste." Retirement planning would be promptly executed and swiftly implemented at the nearest exit.

In a military career, a good "sabbatical" pops up during a 30-day leave. It could happen after retiring from active duty, or after leaving active duty for the Reserves, or even after leaving the service. A similar civilian opportunity is a genuine sabbatical – or even a layoff.

Now that you've read this chapter, **break free of the fog of work**. Take leave and find a way to carve out the time to plan your financial future. Figure out what you like to do, what you need, and when you can start. Stay alert to the opportunities around you – the Reservists at your command, the government employees you work with, or the civilian contractors. They can help with your transition. As you travel the world, learn how other cultures balance living and working and apply these lessons to your situation. Stay in touch with fellow servicemembers who've made the transition, and ask for their help.

Checklist: Just Starting Out

❑ Develop a savings mindset and align your spending with your values.

❑ Start saving early, even if it's "only" $50 per paycheck.

❑ Be frugal where it's valuable, but don't force deprivation on yourself.

❑ Use payroll deductions to automate your savings.

❑ Maximize your contributions to your TSP and your IRAs.

❑ Save a large percentage of your pay raises, promotions, and bonuses.

❑ Consider buying your own home or being a landlord if the lifestyle suits your values, but be aware of the drawbacks.

❑ While you're receiving a military paycheck, consider investing in a more aggressive asset allocation.

❑ Be aware of the "fog of work," and watch your work/life balance.

❑ Review your financial goals and career plans, and contemplate your path to retirement!

Checklist: After Retiring

Ready for life after retirement? This pocket guide lacks the space to cover all the details, but here's the checklist. Visit the website, read the book, or post your own questions at <u>Early-Retirement.org</u>!

- ❏ Now that you're retired, review your goals or changes and plan for the long term – years and decades, not weeks and months.
- ❏ Re-engage with family.
- ❏ Ask yourself every week if you're recreating your old environment.
- ❏ Put away your watch and live at a more leisurely pace.
- ❏ As you develop a retirement routine, pursue your activities when the rest of the world is doing other things.
- ❏ Avoid "retiree guilt."
- ❏ Before you volunteer, figure out how much of your time you want to spend on volunteering.
- ❏ Before you consider a job offer, figure out why you want to work.
- ❏ Explore your financial-management curiosity, but simplify your finances for long-term autopilot.
- ❏ Get healthy and maximize your longevity.
- ❏ Rebel a little, but don't take thoughtless risks.
- ❏ Relax your grooming standards and experiment with new ones.
- ❏ Stop making your bed.
- ❏ Research extended travel options and destinations.
- ❏ If you're feeling restless, consider whether it's being caused by your old lifestyle of changing duty stations every few years.
- ❏ If you're considering school, decide what you want to learn and figure out other ways to learn it. You may not want to subject yourself to the school environment again.

Recommended Reading

This (very) short list was compiled from dozens of veterans and their families. The author has personally read or used all of them and was not bribed to recommend them. Many of them are free through a website or local library. The products are all worth their price, but try the free resources first and see more at www.the-military-guide.com.

Military books:
Armed Forces Guide to Personal Financial Planning
The Military Advantage
The $avvy $ailor and *The $avvy Officer*, by Ralph Nelson

Retirement books:
Work Less, Live More, by Bob Clyatt
The Adventurer's Guide to Early Retirement, by the Kaderlis
Cashing in on the American Dream: How to Retire at 35,
    by the Terhorsts
How to Retire Happy, Wild, and Free, by Ernie Zelinski

Military websites:
www.Military.com
https://staynavytools.bol.navy.mil/RetCalc/Default.aspx
http://www.dfas.mil/militarypay/militarypaytables.html
http://www.tsp.gov/
http://navy.togetherweserved.com/

Retirement websites:
Start at www.The-Military-Guide.com and www.Early-Retirement.org.

Order Form

Full descriptions of the following resources can be found online at www.impactpublications.com or through www.veteransworld.com. Complete this form or list titles, include shipping ($5 plus 10% of the subtotal), enclose payment, and send your order to:

IMPACT PUBLICATIONS
9104-N Manassas Drive
Manassas Park, VA 20111-5211
Tel. 1-800-361-1055, 703-361-7300 or Fax 703-335-9486
Email: query@impactpublications.com

Qty.	Titles	Price	TOTAL
Pocket Guides (quantity discounts on page 60)			
___	Military Family Benefits Pocket Guide	$2.95	___
___	Military Family Education Pocket Guide	2.95	___
___	Military Family Legal Pocket Guide	2.95	___
___	Military Financial Independence & Retirement PG	2.95	___
___	Military Personal Finance Pocket Guide	2.95	___
___	Military Recreation and Travel Pocket Guide	2.95	___
___	Military Spouse's Employment Pocket Guide	2.95	___
___	Military Spouse's Map Through the Maze PG	2.95	___
___	Military-to-Civilian Transition Pocket Guide	2.95	___
___	Military to Federal Government Employment PG	2.95	___
___	The Quick Job Finding Pocket Guide	2.95	___
___	Top Military-Friendly Employers Pocket Guide	2.95	___
___	Veteran's Business Start-Up Pocket Guide	2.95	___
Military Benefits			
___	Claims Denied: How to Appeal a VA Denial	16.95	___
___	Complete Idiot's Guide to Your Military and Veterans Benefits	18.95	___
___	The Military Advantage (annual)	26.95	___
___	Servicemember's Guide to a College Degree	14.95	___
___	Veterans Benefits for Dummies	19.99	___
___	Veteran's Guide to Benefits	16.95	___
___	The Veteran's PTSD Handbook	19.95	___
___	Veteran's Survival Guide	17.95	___

Qty.	Titles	Price	TOTAL
Military Career Transition			
___	Book of U.S. Government Jobs	27.95	___
___	Expert Resumes for Military-to-Civilian Transition	16.95	___
___	Job Search: Marketing Your Military Experience	19.95	___
___	Life After the Military	34.95	___
___	Marketing Yourself for a Second Career DVD	49.95	___
___	Military-to-Civilian Resumes and Letters	21.95	___
___	Military-to-Civilian Transition Guide (annual)	9.95	___
___	Military to Federal Career Guide	18.95	___
___	Military Transition to Civilian Success	21.95	___
Personal Finances, Military Spouses, and Families			
___	Armed Forces Guide to Pers. Financial Planning	22.95	___
___	Best Jobs for Military Spouses	17.95	___
___	Chicken Soup for the Military Wife's Soul	14.95	___
___	Chicken Soup for the Veteran's Soul	14.95	___
___	Complete Idiot's Guide to Life as Military Spouse	12.95	___
___	A Family's Guide to the Military for Dummies	19.99	___
___	Military Spouse Finance Guide	19.95	___
___	Military Spouse's Complete Guide to Career Success	17.95	___
___	Military Spouse's Employment Guide	17.95	___
___	Money Book for the Young, Fabulous, & Broke	16.00	___
___	Today's Military Wife	19.95	___
___	The Truth About Money	19.99	___
Semi-Retirement and Retirement Planning			
___	The AARP Retirement Suvival Guide	14.95	___
___	How to Retire Happy, Wild, and Free	16.95	___
___	Military Guide to Financial Independence and Retirement	17.95	___
___	Retirement Planning Kit (39 books)	685.95	___
___	Work Less, Live More	17.99	___

SUBTOTAL	___
Shipping ($5 + 10% of SUBTOTAL)	___
TOTAL ORDER ------------------------	___